Along My Garden Path

POEMS ON THE RHYTHMS OF LIFE

Holly W Schwartztol

WITH ILLUSTRATIONS BY

Vincent Ostertag

Along My Garden Path: Poems on the Rhythms of Life
Illustrated by Vincent Ostertag
Copyright © 2020 by Holly W. Schwartztol
All rights reserved.

All rights reserved. No part of this book may be used or reproduced by any means, graphic, electronic, or mechanical, including photocopying, recording, taping or by any information storage retrieval system without the written permission of the publisher except in the case of brief quotations embodied in critical articles and reviews.

"Left" and "The Fatal Jump" were published in *Healthy Stories: America's Public Health Literary Journal,* Mami-Dade County Health Department, 2010

"Days Gone By" was published in *The Daily Sun,* October 1, 2016

Several of the poems have appeared in *Author's Voice*, the newsletter of the South Florida Writers Association.

Published by Hallard Press LLC
www.HallardPress.com
Info@HallardPress.com

Bulk copies of this book may be obtained by contacting the author at
drhollyschwartztol@yahoo.com

Cover Design: Hallard Press LLC / John W Prince
Page Design & Typography: Hallard Press LLC / John W Prince
Page Illustrations: Vincent Ostertag

Printed in the United States of America

Library of Congress Control Number: 2020913907

ISBN: 978-1-951188-10-8

010203

What people are saying about
Along My Garden Path.

Her words, these poems, open "portals in the heart" and give us new pathways to each other.
— *Judy Sanger, poet & memoirist*

You are truly gifted… you can move from one to another totally different style seamlessly.—*Dr. June Pimm*

They are nourishing… As varied as they are, the voice is consistent, reliable and intelligent. And sometimes fun.
—*Julie Goldsmith Gilbert, playwright, novelist & biographer*

…simply exquisite. My heart is deeply touched.
—*Sharon Wesch, PhD*

Holly's words on the page evoke nostalgia for what might have been, what we can't fully comprehend, and what we often yearn for. From topics intensely personal to the world we face today, she provides sometimes humorous, sometimes indignant insight.
—*Dr. Barry Morris*

An array of poetry from deeply personal to deeply profound. Wrap your arms around it and enjoy.
—*Patricia Gallant Weich, poet & writer*

DEDICATION

In Memory of
my parents
James and Nancy Wechsler

"The song is ended, but the melody lingers on."
—IRVING BERLIN

Holly W. Schwartztol

Holly W. Schwartztol
Faulkner Creative Writing Competition Awards

2016
Finalist: First Marriage
Semi finalist: Lost Boy

2017
Finalist: Depression Unbound
Semi finalist: Ethics

2018
Finalist: Irreconcilable Differences
      The Madness of Madness
Semi finalist: Missing Judy
      Rather and Father
      The wonder of Birth

2019
Short List: Mixed Emotions prior Trump
Finalist: For My Father, James A. Wechsler
      Special Codes
Semi Finalist: Birthdays
      Dark Side of the Moon
      Dragonfly
      Through Seventy's Eyes

TABLE OF CONTENTS

What people are saying about iii
Dedication v
Faulkner Creative Writing Awards vi
We are Family
    For My Father, James A. Wechsler 2
    Mother's Hands 4
    Lost Boy 6
    For Mother's Christmas 8
    For Our Novelette 9
    My Sons and Their Daughters 17
    I Give Thanks 18
    For Jill 19
Thank You for Being a Friend
    My Odd Friend 22
    A Thousand Lunches and Counting 25
    Another Lost House 29
If I Had a Hammer
    Birthday Blues 34
    Days Gone By 36
    Depression Unbound 38
    Divert Attention 39
    Ethics 40
    Rather and Father 41
    The Fatal Jump 43
    Through Seventy's Eyes 45
        Three Ditties
            The In-Between 46
            Addled 46
            Brain Wise 47
    Strains of Singing Assembly
    (Dalton School, 1950s) 48

We Shall Overcome
- Brief Shining Moment 52
- Mixed Emotion Prior Trump 54
- Our Brave New World 57
- Irreconcilable Differences 58
- If 60
- Dark Side of the Moon 61
- Our Children's Children 62
- Thoughts on Christmas Eve, 2016 63
- Fix the Madness 64
- Will We Ever Learn? 66
- Who Will Win? 69
- The Wonder of Birth 70
- The Hands Lament 72
- Rearranging 74

So Long, Farewell
- For Claire (as she moved from Florida to Seattle) 78
- For Steve W (2013) 81
- For Jeff S, 2013 85
- Not So Easy 88
- Traveling On 90
- First Marriage 92
- House Demolished 95
- Snapshots of Westport 97

Transitions
- Birthdays 102
- Empty 105
- Facebook Angel 107
- For Judy, April 2017 110
- Left 113

    For Franklin Schmidt 1944-2016 116
    Tuesdays at Two 119
    In memory of Latte:
    June 2001 – June, 2016 122

Wonderful, Wonderful

    Appearance 126
    Ella Arrives 127
    Change the World 128
    For Isabella on her first Birthday 131
    Written after seeing the
    Sonogram of Grandchild: 134
    For Baby Grandson Schwartztol 136
    Named in Utero 138

Celebrate Good Things

    When You Just Know 142
    Reunion, 2009 143
    For Carolyn Garwood, PhD,
    On her Retirement 144
    In Love with the Sea 147
    Anniversary 2016 148

Amazing Grace

    Dragonfly 152
    Special Codes 154
    Our Safe Oasis 155
    Lines of Communication 157
    In Another Dimension 159

Acknowledgments 160
About the Author 162
About the Illustrator 163
Other Books by the Author 164

Along My Garden Path

We
Are
Family

Holly W. Schwartztol

For My Father, James A. Wechsler

A writer?
famous?
journalist?
who?

Such a
powerful voice
of the people

Where are
you now?
on the
Other side
in the ethers
somewhere

You shaped
my thoughts
my caring
fostered my
confidence
of expression

Along My Garden Path

You were
a household
name in NYC
among liberal thinkers
and readers
of your pithy
brilliance

Now so many
look quizzically
at me when
I mention your name

Holly W. Schwartztol

Mother's Hands

Nails never painted
on the left hand, a simple gold band
forever youthful

Hands that
combed the knots in my hair -- out
and held the bedtime storybook

A finger outlining the maps of the
cross country trip we once took

Hands forever embedded in my memory
holding hers as we rode to that cemetery

Once to bury my brother, her son
and again my father, her husband

Hands that dug the dirt and planted seeds
in her flower garden then pulled the weeds

The hands that loomed large when mine were small
and seemed to shrink as mine grew

Along My Garden Path

> Hands in the end flailed aimlessly
> when the stroke erased her brain
>
> Hands that yet remain etched within
> my mind reminding me ever
> of her

Holly W. Schwartztol

Lost Boy

Amid echoes of days long past
I'm the lone witness
who speaks of the
lost boy and the family

I'm left here on my own
trying to validate
what happened in
those old broken days

Last I saw you
you were twenty-six
ravaged and torn
asunder by that mind disease

There are no more
parents or aunts
or even loyal friends
... all now gone

To help me discern
what made you turn
from the brilliant
friendly and caring

Totally sane young boy
into the one
whose last years
knew too many wards

No one left to help
sort out what
really happened
was it the LSD?

Or some genetic
mutation that
robbed you of
your you-ness

Choosing to end
your sad existence
with a bottle of
pills leaving you

     gone
from all understanding
for our mother to discover
your lifeless body

On that sunny May morning
with spring kissing the air
as you drifted
away from us all

Holly W. Schwartztol

For Mother's Christmas

Every year I swore
I'd get home to New York for your Christmas fete

To mingle with those folks who came year
after year as one close group merry at your table

 Did I really think
you'd never leave us?
that time would wait?

For me to fly to your door to celebrate
the winter solstice and Christmas cheer

I'll rely on childhood memories of Christmases past
the tree we'd lug home on Christmas eve
to hang those precious Santas, balls and tinsel
and watch as those colored lights
came on and we sang our carols and Tom Lehrer

How I wish I'd gone when you were here
welcoming those who did come
and share and who I know are
also missing those nights you gave
every blessed year

Every year I swore
I'd get home to New York

FOR OUR NOVELETTE

Where to
begin to
tell the
story of
our Nov?
The lithe young thing
who arrived on
March 29, 1981
to care
for
our
small boy,
Laurence.

Like a soft
wind from
Jamaica she
quietly came
to organize
our household
and walked
directly into
the core of
our young
family.

Holly W. Schwartztol

She sometimes
spoke of
odd things
like saying
that the
bird at the
window was
a family member
who had died
long before
my consciousness
evolved to
Nov's way
of thinking…

Nov chatted
easily with
my father
and they
shared views
on everything
from politics
to basketball
and every
other sport.

Along My Garden Path

In March
of 1982
when baby Andrew
was born
we brought
him home and
handed him
to Nov's
waiting arms
and she promptly
bathed him in
the bathroom sink.

She loved
my mother
too who
she called
"My favorite lady"
Their closeness
was warm
and deep

We mourned
together the
dark year of
1983 when
her beloved
daughter, Bonnie

Holly W. Schwartztol

was senselessly
killed while
driving with
her sister, Diana
as they drove
preparing for
Bonnie's wedding

A life cut
down by a
Metro bus
at a stop
Sign.

And, then
not six
months later
when lung
cancer claimed
my father's life
from the
deadly cigarettes
he'd smoked
for over forty
years, Nov
mourned with
us.

Nov spent
so many
evenings in
deep conversation
with Jill
about what
hopes Nov
had and
whether she
would remain
in our house
or seek
employment elsewhere;
a chat
I quickly
hushed.

And
of course
Nov came to
us not
alone
but in
the company
of her
dear husband
Dudley who
lovingly tended
our gardens

Holly W. Schwartztol

from house to
house and even
drove Nov
downtown after
we moved to
Brickell Key
until we
lost him
to those
ugly cigarettes
as well.

Nov shared
all our joys
as well
and every
little thing
which has
transpired in
our home
She was
there to welcome
me as
Dr Holly
who Larry
called Dr. Mommy
and to
celebrate Bar Mitzvahs
and engagements
marriages
and births.

Nov's wisdom
included saying
how when
one door closes
another door
opens.

And she
opined how
"money make
friend and
money break friend."

And as
the years
went by
we knew
that these
earthy truths
were so
right on.

We do
not know how
we are
going to
be able
to say
Good bye

Holly W. Schwartztol

> to our
> dearest friend
> and so
> we will
> just say
> so long
> for now
> until we
> meet again
> in the very
> near time
> when she will
> journey to
> our new home
> where we
> will welcome
> her as an
> honored guest.

My Sons and Their Daughters

Watching each of my sons
as they parent their daughters
my heart opens wide
it's like drinking clear waters

With tenderness
patience and awe
seemingly with little stress
I watch them as they

Champion their girls
and hold them in such esteem
we must have done something right
to realize this poignant dream

For this old mommy
nothing could be more sweet
than to witness these men
accomplish such a feat.

Holly W. Schwartztol

I Give Thanks

Perhaps it's an old sorry tale
how 'a son is a son till he takes a wife'
and I've heard gruesome stories
as I've traveled through this life

Of problems with in-law children
causing so much strain
and moms of sons
often repeat a sad refrain.

And this is why I give thanks
as my sons both chose to marry
women I cherish so dearly
so the old tale doesn't carry

Any weight in our family
as we delight in the two
and count our blessings
in all that they do.

For Jill

When we met in '75
you were merely eight years old
lucky was I to be alive
and have you to behold

You dazzled me with your beautiful smile
your intelligence and wit
I was absolutely beyond beguiled
and loved you every little bit

My mind was in such a whirl
loving your dad from the first
and here you were his little girl
my heart surely did almost burst

My dearest Jill, it's about time
way beyond our kinship
to let you know inside this rhyme
how I so cherish your friendship

$V = 切片$

Thank You for Being a Friend

Holly W. Schwartztol

My odd friend

Railroad train was late that day
filled the hours chatting
with strangers

A dark-haired woman
never saw again
and the handsome man

In a three-piece suit
with a quick wit
And a winning smile

Met him a week later
train more timely
yakked all the way

From Port Jefferson
to New York City
invited him to dine

Soon with my husband
and with me
he became nearly family

Along My Garden Path

Lived in odd house
at top of a hill
alone with a new dog

We didn't see things
in same way
yet enjoyed sharing

Different aspects of
government and politics
neither of us

Liked the President
It was 1969
he came into my life

As I was about
to lose my brother
and he filled in

A space in my
heart where no
one else could

Holly W. Schwartztol

Through the years
others saw him
as strange

Yet we've maintained
the connection over
half a century

He married for a time
had two children
with whom he has little

Relationship as of now
and we merely speak
we've not seen one another

In over fifteen years
yet when we speak
he's 28 again

And I'm 22
and we carry on
the conversation

that we began as
strangers on a train

A Thousand Lunches and Counting
1984—2011

We said we'd lunch
every Monday
unless one of us
was out of town
or at a funeral

We never let
another soul
dine with us
and interfere
with our
cherished schedule
meeting just us two

Our husbands asked
what do you speak
about at those
private lunches of yours?

Mine thought he'd
be the subject
and longed to be
the proverbial
fly upon the wall

Holly W. Schwartztol

And, yes, at times
we spoke of
husbands or children
or friends
because you see
we spoke of all
that mattered
most to us

Because we knew
that everything
was safe and sound
with the other
A treasured friendship
that grew more
dear for every year

We cried when we lost
our fathers
and our mothers
and some friends
and a sister-in-law

Sometimes we just
spoke of the
books we read
and other times
of the movies
we'd seen that week

Along My Garden Path

Rarely though was
there a lunch
with a lull in
conversation

We frequented
restaurants week
after week
until something
left us wanting

And then we
found another place

We lost and
gained a
thousand pounds
from OA to Weight
Watchers to South
Beach and beyond
always celebrating
each other
and, silly me
I so believed
we'd grow old
together

Eating lunch
every Monday
somewhere
together

Holly W. Schwartztol

Only now you
are moving
far away from me
You never said
you'd make that choice
leaving me with
empty Mondays
at lonely restaurants
searching for
my friend.

Another Lost House

Lazy afternoons with my darling friend
   in the charming house
      overlooking Biscayne Bay

We talked
  we listened
     played scrabble

Petted the lovely large dog
  sipped iced tea
     delighted in one another

Through the Clinton and Bush Years
  we marveled
    then grimaced

Holly W. Schwartztol

Then I moved out of town
  a few years later
    more changes

Her house was sold
  then taken down
    not even replaced

Leaving a gaping hole
  where once the
    stately house had stood

My friend and I still speak
  through the miles
    on the telephone

And over lunch
  when I'm in town
    visiting Miami

Along My Garden Path

    She lives in another
       lovely home
          and another large dog

    Oversees our games and talks
       yet the house on the water
          still calls to me

    And fills my heart with longing

If I Had a Hammer

Holly W. Schwartztol

Birthday Blues

Every year I notice
those who call
and write
or post
the folks who
drop by
to wish
me the best

I know I should
only focus
on those
who do
remember to
recognize
 my special day.

Just as I reach out
to them on
their birthdays
and other
special occasions.
Perhaps it's a
throw-back to
childhood parties
waiting for
friends to
appear at my door

Along My Garden Path

That brings the old
yearning and
longing for those
who somehow let
my birthday
slip by without
the call or the
note or
even the
post....

So if it is you
who forgets to
smile upon your
friends or relations
let this be
a wake-up
call and be
sure to reach
out and not
let the day
come to a
close without
your hello

Holly W. Schwartztol

Days Gone By

Remember when the web
belonged to spiders
and the internet
had no riders?

And cells belonged
to science
not a dialed
appliance?

We learned about
the birds and bees
not how we should
replace our knees

Set our hair
in rollers
not how to implant
new molars

Kept our shoes on
when we flew
brought our water
by the crew

Along My Garden Path

We worried then
about our taxes
no one heard
of writing faxes

Phone calls were often missed
we traded sexy looks
made eye contact when we spoke
saved texts for our school books

Movies were viewed in theaters
not in our homes
or heaven forfend on
our portable phones

With all these new gadgets
our lives are much fleeter
yet I yearn for days past
when time seemed much sweeter

Holly W. Schwartztol

Depression Unbound

He cries out
his undampened pain
his unmitigated angst
like relentless drops of rain

I hear his long lament
and feel my heart strain
yet nothing I have to offer
softens his grim refrain

Humpty Dumpty's famous fall
holds no candle to his sorrow
and I, like all those Kings' Men,
can't give him a bright tomorrow.

DIVERT ATTENTION

My morning self-directive
is keep a wide perspective
lest I drown in all we fear
there's much I hold dear

Baby Billie claps and dances
what may be the chances
her precocious attention
to rhythm I must mention

Everyone who sees her antics
wastes no semantics
we're all so much in awe
she takes after her paw

This one-year old cutie
and really such a beauty
has captured our hearts
she's really off the charts

So though the world this minute
has scary stories in it
I'll choose to turn my gaze
toward our Billie's happy days

Holly W. Schwartztol

ETHICS

Is it truly antithetical
to live a life that's ethical?
In a world of texting
and sexting
where technology
invades the psychology
of how we relate
and how we create
new pathways to
each other?

Will the old
rules suffice or
do we need
new advice
a new fashion
about how to live
with fairness
integrity
and compassion?

Rather and Father

Is it too far of a stretch
for me to create a sketch
between the word Rather
and the one who was my father?

Hoping poetic license
in the truest sense
gives me permission
for this mission

The journalists two
are Dan Rather
and James A.
Wechsler my father.

Both born on Halloween
James in 1915
Daniel in 1931
serendipity always such fun!

Both of these men
with excellent pen
from a classic Royal
and now a Facebook loyal

Holly W. Schwartztol

Did they know
one another
back in the day
I really can't say

But both are champion
of values I cherish
cut from similar cloth
determined we not perish

From misguided fools
such as Nixon and Trump
who preside as ghouls
turning America into a sump

We turn to James and Dan
for wisdom and candor
their voices the ages span
protecting us from those who pander

To diminished government
and assured internment
losing our ideals
amid dishonest appeals

It's surely no mystery
through each stage of history
that articulate writers
are our very best fighters

THE FATAL JUMP

Who hasn't paused
and wondered at times?
lingering at the edge
of the high window ledge

What would happen if
 you leaned out too far
and suddenly slipped
as your mind simply flipped

And yet knowing somehow
how you'd resist that urge
and perhaps move away
from temptation's sway

I reel back in shock
of that stranger's strange choice
was she stoned on meth
as she fell to her death?

Splattered by the valet
for all to encounter
brains spilled on the street
blood at our feet

Holly W. Schwartztol

Piercing the day
with no thought of who'd see
she got out of her life
gave up on her strife

But left us all alone
wondering what we will do
with nightmarish frights
of what falls from these heights

Through Seventy's Eyes

Inside thoughts could be twenty-five
though seven decades I've been alive
watching people who're nearing thirty
it won't do for me to be flirty

But tell that to my brain
or my friend who sports a cane
why does the world not see
we're still the younger we

The mirrors may reveal
lines I'd rather conceal
I claim the light's not right
and disregard this sight

This thing's as old as time
and fitting for this rhyme
inside I'm not so old
I've stories to be told

Holly W. Schwartztol

Three Ditties

The In-Between

Afternoon the in-between
the client yet to come
my desk should be
a sight unseen
I pour myself some tea

Will my focus have the knack
when she sits with me
will all my know how
bring gladness back
and gently soothe her now?

Addled

All of my gadgets
addle my brain
I'm kindled
blackberried
and skyped
For my pain

Brain Wise

They say the
brain's plastic
my tissues can stretch
and learning Chinese
will keep me on target

No more will I
search for
word lost in thought
I'm busily learning how
not to forget!

Holly W. Schwartztol

STRAINS OF SINGING ASSEMBLY (DALTON SCHOOL, 1950s)

It's a me,
It's a me,
It's a me, oh lord
standing in the
need of Prayer....

A mighty fortress
is our God
a bulwark
never failing

Tiritomba!
Tiritomba!
All the world
is calling
calling to me now

We gather together
to ask the lords blessing
He hastens and chastens
our will to make known

Along My Garden Path

The golden sun is setting
beyond the woodland hill
...the toil of day is over
and field and flock are still

Do-o na no-o bis
pachem, pachem
do oh na-a
no-bis
pa-a-a
a-chem

Who is Sylvia?
what is she-e?
that all her
swains commend her?

Singing together
we went forth unafraid

We Shall
Overcome

Holly W. Schwartztol

Brief Shining Moment

Bursting with pride
was I on
January 20, 2009
as Barack Obama
and Michelle
became our
First family.

So thankful am
I for eight years
of class and compassion
gentility and grace
of articulate leaders
who inspired hope
and made me so
immensely proud
to be an
American living in this
time of the
best of us.

Whatever follows
will never erase
the outstanding
years of tenderness
and sunlight
these two wise and
brilliant souls
gave this
country.

So, I say
thank you
to the fates
that allowed
me to be
on this earth
during these amazing
if brief
shining moments.

Holly W. Schwartztol

MIXED EMOTION PRIOR TRUMP

So much to hold
all at once
to celebrate this 27th day
of June 2015
Latte's 70th birthday—cat years
gay marriage legal across the land
ObamaCare upheld

And then that
sadness knowing
just one year
ago today my
friend, Al Brown
left this earth.

From the killings in
Charleston comes
the unity of our
best selves
and our president's
most eloquent remarks
asking us to
take action and not
just talk about gun sense

Along My Garden Path

The heart
makes room
for it all

The wonder of
some progress
at last in a world
so often filled
with horror
and mayhem
more terrorism
in Europe just
Yesterday...

Yet, my dear cat
will welcome guests
tonight to toast
her furriness
and goodness

And the Supreme Court
earned that adjective
with its superb rulings
amid all the turmoil
and duality of human
interaction

Holly W. Schwartztol

And we will
see how we
can hold all
these feelings together

The joy
the silliness
the pride
the sadness

I honor each
separate feeling
as I pause to
let my heart stretch
just a little bit more.

Our Brave New World

Everywhere you look
everyone's a crook
in this new world
we've simply been took

The wisest of the bunch
are all out to lunch
bankers, czars of finance
in this dreadful crunch

Where are we to turn
what else will we learn?
each day's news leaves
us with more heartburn

Holly W. Schwartztol

Irreconcilable Differences

We share the same block
palm trees grace our yards
we bask in the same
Florida sunshine
play golf and Mah Jong

And there
all similarity ends
"Don't discuss politics"
is the mantra
and now I
fully see why

My ears imploded with
"There are some good Nazis"
"Obama was a terrible speaker; he started all
sentences with er..."

"If Trump talks down to women
it's because of how women dress"
"If democrats want to
help the poor why don't they
give their money to them?"
"Women hang all over Trump
and then scream harassment
when he rejects them"

"I hate the dreamers!"

These wretched lines
filled the air at
Christmas no less
from neighbors who
didn't even
notice they were
addressing two liberal Jews

How do I reconcile
living among those
whose values are
so diametrically
opposed to all
Decency in the world?

The wine flowed
turkey and ham
and stuffing
and corn
while the conversation
was political porn

Holly W. Schwartztol

If

If we don't all get the corona virus
if the icebergs
stop melting
If Trump doesn't get reelected
or refuse to leave when someone else wins

I might be able to breathe
I might be able to sleep

Dark Side of the Moon

China lands on dark
side of the moon
we're being run
by a darkened loon.

World spinning
round in shock
to see America
run by such schlock

2019 on day number three
we're rocketing down
no end in sight
will democracy drown?

Holly W. Schwartztol

Our Children's Children

What good is money
and power if we
can't drink our water
or breathe our air?

Is this some nightmare?
some part of delirium?
will I wake up and find
it's all fake news?

That the powers that be
really want my children's
children to live in a
world where honesty

And compassion still
have meaning and where
government, per Elizabeth
Warren works for the people?

Or will we burn in
the man-made hell
we've created and lose
the country we call home?

Thoughts on Christmas Eve, 2016

Used to love the morning *Times*
now I'll stick to fun and rhymes
cause every story has lost its glory

The globe is rattling with fear all over
leaving me battling and running for cover
will we survive and stay alive
with every country shivering
against the tide of unrest
I feel a quivering where
I once felt hope and glee
wondering what will be
our ultimate destiny?

Holly W. Schwartztol

Fix the Madness

Must have been
how they felt on
the Titanic
with the water washing
over the sides of
the mighty ship.

No way to stop
the destruction
no way out
no one to right
the ship and
send it back
on its course.

Along My Garden Path

Who will fix
the madness
of this
Trumped up
disastrous charge
toward the
loss of our America?

We must find
a way to
bring the
scales of justice
back into balance
And we must do
It now!

Holly W. Schwartztol

Will We Ever Learn?

Strains of Turn Turn Turn
play on my Amazon Prime
as I weep for the world
we find ourselves in.

"A time for peace,
I swear it's not too late...."
and I truly wonder
if that's so.

I suppose our parents
felt this way when
the atrocities of
world War II were
uncovered.

Is it so much
to ask
to wonder
when we will
ever learn?

When the
despicable killings
will cease?
Beheadings in the
21st Century?

And then I'm
reminded how
at the most basic
level we are all one...

What is it that
provokes these horrors to
continue day after day
when the morning news
is more than I can stand?

And it goes on
all day every day
I change radio stations
play music on the t.v.
to block out the
terror of this world.

But my heart shatters
each time another
report comes through
when even in Oklahoma
a beheading occurs.

When disease erupts in
Africa killing so many
innocents and now
invades a Texas town.

Holly W. Schwartztol

And, then I am told
to turn my focus away
from the madness
so I won't attract
the insanity to continue.

Where in that
is my responsibility to
reach out and shed
 this helplessness that
I feel?

Who will Win?

We've come to this standstill
feeling like part of a landfill
all nations stand at attention
is this a divine intervention?

While we debated climate change
still ten years in the offing
our plans must rearrange
since we've started coughing

It's something microscopic
and the only current topic
it's brought us to our knees
it's not a simple tease

Our country strains
from Donald Trump's refrains
he commands loyalty as he
thinks himself royalty

The world's spinning out of whack
while we're ruled by a decadent hack
will the virulent virus win
while we listen to his spin?

Holly W. Schwartztol

The Wonder of Birth

The wonder of birth
your baby so sweet
brings unequaled mirth
born of passion and heat

Becoming a toddler
discovering butterflies
you are her coddler
watching her happy feet rise

She waves to you as she
enters school the first time
she'll learn to read and write
you see her inner light

There'll be some good times
some struggles too
but always at night
she'll return home to you.

There are dangers to fear
you teach her safety rules
she's still your most dear
surely, she's safe at school

On Valentine's day
celebrating love is cool
what did the news say?
a gunman loose at her school?
She's got be okay
she'll have protection
she'll flee far away
and find a connection

The news report booms
the gunman's prey are splattered
in hallways and classrooms
her tender life is shattered

Holly W. Schwartztol

The Hands Lament

We've been everywhere you've gone
foreign shores and grocery stores
from dusk to dawn
and all your chores

From your morning shower
to preparing for your bed
we've never seen you cower
with so much germy dread

As a child you'd wash us
before a meal
or your mom would fuss
and make a big deal

We look at you with wonder
now you wield soap
from home to yonder
and wonder how you'll cope

You must not touch your face
you mustn't share a hug
you wash us every place
you might catch a nasty bug

So we ask you dear Holly
we your trusted hands
is this just folly
can we meet your new demands

As the virus lurks around
on metal and fabric and doors
we gaze up as you've found
ways to clean out all the spores!

Holly W. Schwartztol

Rearranging

Our grandson is caring and so bright
converses about matters of state
outspoken, shines his light
ready to go through the gate

He will fight for human rights
in his school and for the nation
studies late into the nights
even on some vacation

Graduated last year
ready to leave the town
his fate he'd easily steer
nothing would keep him down.

Entered Cornell this fall
took to the college life
what could cause a stall
fate struck like a knife

 Covid-19 invaded the world
halting everything in its path
all plans became unfurled
with this virus' wrath

Along My Garden Path

No one knows what's next
what colleges will do
just know our moods are vexed
till a vaccine wipes out this flu.

Our Sam is very clever
he'll find an innovation
and unearth an endeavor
to overcome the frustration.

So Long, Farewell

Holly W. Schwartztol

For Claire
(as she moved from Florida to Seattle)

When did I say
it would ever be okay
for you to leave?

How do we let go
of all the years
and all we've known

From bliss to
heartache and back again
we've seen it all

Though I know
we'll always be close
I wanted you to stay

And remain where I am
for all the coming years
of dinners and lunches

and knowing you'd be
right where I could
Find you?

Along My Garden Path

Fate robbed you of your sight
and now steals you from mine
and I'm just not ready

For you to move clear
across this vast country
to another world

And though I know
you had little choice
and ultimately this

Will most likely be
a good move for you
and maybe I'll learn

To accept that you
just don't live here anymore
but I'm not there yet

I want to hold onto you
and keep you from going
and keep you near

Holly W. Schwartztol

Is this a poem?
or something else?
Does it convey

The sense of loss
and deep sadness
I am feeling?

In this week of Thanksgiving
as you fly away
carrying my heart

For Steve W (2013)

Music
Hypnosis
even Neurofeedback
long drives
to conferences
constant debate
about why
we are
who we
are and
where we are
going
long talks about
everything
that matters
How do we
sum
up
thirty years
of
deep attachment?

Holly W. Schwartztol

Excitement of
learning new
ways to help
our clients
always eager
to pursue
even when
it meant
we swam
upstream

From the years
sipping Scotch
to Vodka
Cosmos
or hypnotic trances
from Canada
to Cleveland
to Ft Myers
Melbourne
even Key Largo

Those long
talks and
quests to
discover all
that we do

New Years
fireworks over
Biscayne Bay
you strumming
your guitar
singing of
being Just
A child

You've touched
my heart and
played such
a large part
in so many
nooks and crannies

Of my life
and leaving
you now
feels
somehow
unfair and
out of sync

Will skype
and email
telephones
or snail mail
assuage the

Holly W. Schwartztol

loss of
seeing you
so many
days of so
many weeks?

Yet hearts that
connect
remain
together
no
matter
where we
live

So, I'll
count on that
and carry
your essence
with me
to
The Villages
and beyond

Along My Garden Path

For Jeff S, 2013

How I will miss you
When I hear
a Broadway
song I'll
miss our
sing-alongs
when new
challenges tax
my aging mind
and I just
don't get the
gist of what
I'm supposed
to know so
quickly
I'll miss
your knowing
glance that
says you
understand
my angst.

When a
dragonfly
appears out
of the
blue and I
know it

Holly W. Schwartztol

has a message
I'll miss
how you
never judge
my trust
in the
unseen.

It has
indeed been
a wondrous
journey filled
with learning
growing and
sharing giggles
on our
walks
to Scully's
and beyond.
I'll miss
Our endless
chats and
easy access
your office
just a
few steps
from mine;
your tolerance
of my
interruptions

of your
case notes.

So much
will I miss
it boggles
my brain
and in
my heart
I feel
a pull
to see
you more
again.

Yes, we
do have
email
and Skype
and electronic
means of
closeness
but it
just isn't
the same
and so
I will miss
you
more than
you could
know.

Holly W. Schwartztol

Not So Easy

We learn to love
We learn to connect
then we're told
it's better not to
hold on
but
to
let
go

Better to have no
expectations
to know that
the
only
sure thing
is
change

We raise
our children
so
they
Can fly away
to be
independent

We love our
friends and

yet we
sometimes choose
to journey away
to find
new landscapes
and try
our own
wings

It all
seems so
sound and
adult but
holding on
is what we've
learned and
it isn't
easy
to
fly

Pulled toward
the new and
the different
yet wanting
to preserve
all
that
we
have
known

Holly W. Schwartztol

Traveling On

I don't have to hate it here
to love it there
from the arching trees
on Old Cutler Road
to the vista of
ocean and bay
on the bridge to
Key Biscayne
from tree lined
streets of Coral Gables
and Coconut Grove
buildings reaching for the
open sky on Brickell

Dear friends from forty years
of living and growing
in South Florida
my colleagues and clients
writer's Club
book Club
singing in temple choirs
you will all be in my heart

Along My Garden Path

> As I journey a bit North
> to rolling hills and new
> beginnings with some
> old friends and some new
> a gentler life
> reminiscent of Miami
> as she was when first
> I found her

Holly W. Schwartztol

First Marriage

You invited me to view
the computerized slide show
you fashioned from old pictures
of shared living and being

Landscapes and brilliant sunsets
bridges famous and not
old explored terrain
we ventured toward

From Port Jefferson, L.A. and Venice
Yosemite, Martinique and Rome
timeless snapshots
spiraling through decades

Mountains grand and soaring
rugged coastal highways
fragrant whiffs of pine
and open skies

The friends, some true
some false
peer out at us
some now nearly unrecognizable
in 70's garb

Along My Garden Path

And animals who witnessed
those student days of old
they gave us all their
love and matchless trust

Our orange cat sitting
side by side with
our gray tabby
gazing through windows

The cats, always intuiting
what perhaps eluded
our so called insights
and imaginings

Those two young souls you and I
spinning through time and space
we who thought
we knew everything

A portal in my heart
allows a sudden rush
of ancient inklings
tinges of forgotten textures

Holly W. Schwartztol

Remembered scents
and wonderings
of the girl I'd been
thinking herself a woman

Your narrative was tender
observations so sweet
as you spoke of those
days of youth so far away

It's over forty years
we've created other lives
with those we cherish
and hold so very dear

Yet, for those brief moments
our memories transported
us and we recalled
such fun that we once were

House Demolished

Yes, we must
Accept change
and let the
fates
rearrange
what
once
we held so dear.

A house sold
and all my
rights to its
future
voided
so
quickly
by the bye.

The striking
image of
the beloved
home of
my childhood
and beyond
so violently
demolished
by the uncaring

Holly W. Schwartztol

> ravaging machine
> haunts my
> thoughts
> and renders
> me similarly
> torn
>
> My insides turn
> and twist
> as I recall
> the sundering of
> 40 Danbury
> I cry against
> the reality
> of a new
> house standing
> on that sacred
> ground.

SNAPSHOTS OF WESTPORT

Paned windows looking over
the soft green summer grass
every summer of my life.

The latched door
leading down carpeted
stairs to the side door

Comfy couches
floor lamps
A wooden closet

All built so we
could have private
moments by ourselves

A choice to
crawl thru the tiny door
like Alice in Wonderland

Leading to a guest room
with so many windows
overlooking the graveled driveway

Holly W. Schwartztol

Painted wooden floor
an easel left from
when the little boy

Once slept there
or harkening even
further back

To sleepovers shared
with best friends
visiting me for weekends

So many memories
etched forever in
my heart which longs

For a house
that was sold
and then torn down

For Westport summers
and loving parents
who've left this earth

Visions of a time
and place remain
indelibly in my mind

Transitions

Holly W. Schwartztol

Birthdays

Birthdays celebrate personhood
and all my life
if you've told me
when yours is
I tend to remember the date.

I may not have seen
you for decades
you may not even
remember my name
but your birthday
remains in my brain.

So, today on February 25th
I thought of
my old friend Al Brown.
and Googled the
man hoping to find
where he lives
these days.

A contact with him
nigh near ten years
allowed us to share
and catch up on

careers, marriages,
our children
his retirement from
Psychology to Maine.
He told me
he'd survived a
bout with tongue cancer...

Over the years,
when I was able
I'd send him a
greeting as
February waned.

He seemed to
appreciate my
caring to send
my very best
as it's said.

But Google
has given me pause
today, as I
sadly discovered
that my Alan Brown
did not reach this
birthday, that he died
end of last June.

Holly W. Schwartztol

> I never knew he was born in Manhattan…
>
> My heart is
> saddened to learn
> of his passing.
> I hope it was easy
> they say he died surrounded
> by his family.

Empty

My rudder
is disconnected
as if the me
you birthed
and raised
is set adrift

The world
has lost
the safety net
which always
said that
I was still
someone's child

Now I'm
the one
the children
seek for their support
and comfort

And I'm
Grandma Golly
and Dr Holly
and someone's wife
And I'm the

Holly W. Schwartztol

older one
that others
look to for
their security

Where did you
go when
summer reached
it's height?
I search amid
empty houses
lawyers' offices
old landscapes

Whose barren shores
evoke that
empty place
inside my heart
and force me to march on
without your guidance
and wise counsel

Facebook Angel

How many times
do I need to learn
of a death
on Facebook?

Scrolling merrily
down a page
only to be
clobbered with

news so shocking

This week a
friend's son
posted that his
father became an angel
last week.

But how can that be
I just spoke with his
mother two weeks ago
his father was to
have a small surgery

Holly W. Schwartztol

The small obit
in *The New York Times*
I missed on the one
day that my husband
threw the paper out
before I got to read it

I'd have visited
my friend that day
we were in New York
and now we are
back in Florida
and it's too late

My heart truly hurts
for my dear friend, Pat
we've known each other since our
teens, even dated the same boy
for a while

We've been there for each other
her mother's untimely death in 1965
and then my father's
she came to my mother's funeral in 09

We seem to meet at funerals
or to mark these major losses
her voice still sounds exactly
as it did over fifty years ago

Only now she's not
answering her phone
I've messaged her son
on his Facebook page
and privately as well

But I need to hear
Pat's voice and let
her know I'm here for
her to soothe her
troubled heart

She's been through
so much in recent years
she's tired
said so much
had happened that she
wondered if they'd make it

And now Martin is gone
surely a major angel
as his son Graig said
and I hope to hold Pat's hand
and help her through
this terrible time

Holly W. Schwartztol

For Judy, April 2017

If love could heal
cancer
you'd be home
in your life

I call you and
we're indignant
at all the
pieces of
your living
with this
unspeakable horror

Losing your hair
your "oneliness"
being shunted
from place to place

Those whose words
pierce your heart
rendering you even
more vulnerable

Along My Garden Path

> To the pain
> and the invasion
> of this disease
> which threatens
> to rob you of
> your sense of
> self.
>
> You feel punished
> isolated from those
> who claim to
> love you
>
> Who can't
> see their way
> to journey
> to your side
>
> Who find reasons
> why this time
> and that week
> won't work

Holly W. Schwartztol

For them
to fly to you
and hold your hand
and who

Don't understand
why you seem
so unappreciative
of what they've

Done so far
and who also
feel utterly
helpless to

Meet your needs
at this most
excruciating time
of aloneness

And sickness
and incredible
challenge to
everything that

you hold dear.

LEFT

Early on that morning
I wracked my brain
trying to solve
a computer glitch

As I left the wretched machine
I rose and felt suddenly dizzy
and as the room spun

I chided myself
saying this isn't worth
your having a stroke

I lay down on the bed
listened to a disc
that promised
relaxation and rest

My head stopped throbbing
and the phone rang
the caller ID said
Mother

What was she doing at
home in mid-morning?
only the voice on
the other end
wasn't hers

Holly W. Schwartztol

But the
maid I'd never met
telling me of mother's
neck pain and strange speech

And then I knew
that my pain had
really belonged to her

That my dizziness
reflected hers and that
it was she who was
in fact, having a stroke

Frantic calls ensued
between Miami and New York
a neurologist
saying how the stroke

Had been massive
and the prognosis was grim
words of paralysis
and irretrievable
brain damage

I faxed the living will
which is really the
will of the living isn't it?

We sat by her bedside
for four endless days
and then her breath
was no more and she was gone.

And at 62 I was
suddenly an orphan
both parents gone
the older brother
having gone 40 years ago

How do I live in
this world
on this planet
as the lonely satellite

The last member
of my nuclear family
here to sift through
the pictures

And the letters
and all the memorabilia that
make up a life

Holly W. Schwartztol

For Franklin Schmidt 1944-2016

You were part
of the fabric
of my youth

The day you
and your brother
Michael entered the
ballroom at Viola Wolff's
Dancing School is
crystal clear to me
though that was
well over half
a century ago

You two handsome
dark haired young
men were a dashing
vision to this
thirteen year
old young girl.
We three spent
many years dancing
and playing at
all those youthful
emotions.

Along My Garden Path

You wrote poems
to wit:
"The winds of love
Sang to me
They whispered softly
Stephanie"
and
'neuroses, neuroses
in dozens and grosses"

At least those snippets
are what I recall
along with fleeting
images of 450 West End Avenue
or getting lost driving to Westport
your interest in journalism

I'm not the first
to ask
where does the time go?

I walked this afternoon
thinking of you
and a small bird
perched upon a
road sign.

Holly W. Schwartztol

I took this
as a message
from you from
the world beyond
where I know
you are safe
and out of pain.

And where I
trust I will
see you one
day again.

Tuesdays at Two

You are irreplaceable
my Tuesdays at two
elegance and warmth
filling the room

Always open to
discover what
new perception
would enhance your life.

Year after year
sharing your
thoughts and innermost
feelings always

Seeking to
find new answers
to old questions
about your worth

Of who you are
despite all
evidence from
so many

Holly W. Schwartztol

Of your unique
intelligence and
talents, your caring
for those you loved

Open to my take
on whatever
might be troubling you
seeking the messages

You sought
to uncover
and learn about
yourself and your world.

I was privileged
to receive and share
you through
these magical years

To help you sort
out your truth
as I learned so
much from you.

Yesterday, on Tuesday at
Two you were
honored by so many

Along My Garden Path

> Who will as I
> miss your presence
> on this plane
> in this dimension
> until we meet again.

Holly W. Schwartztol

In memory of Latte: June, 2001 – June, 2016

Every place in our home
holds the essence of
our beloved Birman
cat, Latte.

From the chairs out on
the lanai where she'd
bask in the sunlight

Or peer out
from the covers
of our bed.
She'd jump up on every
counter top
find a nesting place
on a closet shelf
or in a bathroom drawer

Latte greeted us when
we came in by
lolling across the top
of the couch or a chair
She'd meow loudly at me
cautioning me to turn
off the computer by 10:30
p.m. and come to bed.

Along My Garden Path

Sometimes for no
earthly reason, she'd howl
plaintively at us
or plant herself right in
front of the monitor as I
wrote my books and poems.

She was the most
beautiful cat with paws
resembling a French
manicure and silky
hair of shades of brown,
white and cream.

She never heard how
cats are supposed to be aloof
and so would snuggle up
with us, fixing her deep blue eyes on
us or just nuzzling against our chests.

And though her energy
lingers in the ethers of
our home,
nothing will ever replace
the soft, delicious kitty
who gave us her heart
and stole ours forever.

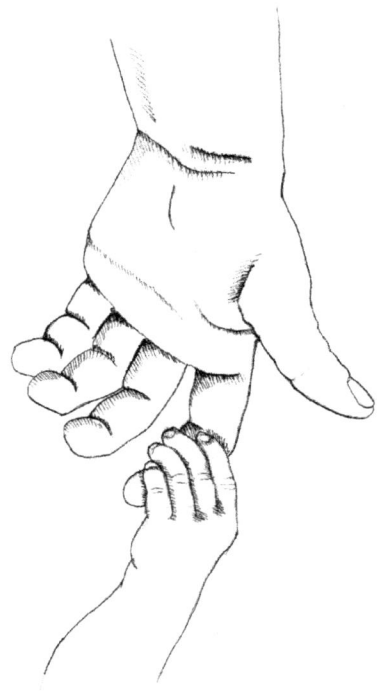

Wonderful, Wonderful

Holly W. Schwartztol

Appearance

The call came late at night
gave us a bit of a fright

Perhaps it's a kidney stone
causing her to moan and groan
but actually what's happened
got us all a-clappin'

When Jill's proverbial water released
and much of our worrying ceased
it seems grandbaby Sam
decided hot damn

He'd make his appearance
without the usual clearance

Ella Arrives

Baby's coming today
Jill will want food when she's done
to the deli we made our way
anticipating lots of fun

Expecting a long wait
we trooped in before too long
found John at the gate
had something gone wrong?

We couldn't contemplate
why he wasn't at his wife's side
until we heard him joyously state
with a grin mighty wide

"Twenty minutes ago your daughter
brought forth a surprise
gave birth to your granddaughter!"
happy tears fell from our eyes

And that is how shortly after her birth
our Ella left nothing to chance
when she'd arrived here on this earth
to join the family's dance

Holly W. Schwartztol

Change the World

The grandbaby
moved today
inside her mother

On this day
when the
cowardly senate

Failed to pass
background checks
for gun owners

In a week
when runners
were maimed
and killed
by another lunatic
and letters
laced with
poison
were sent
to government
leaders

Along My Garden Path

The baby moved
today as her
assuring us
of her
presence

Let this
dear grand
daughter for
whom we
all await
in total love

Find a world
that honors
peace and
justice and
caring

Grandest
Grand
daughter
we will

Holly W. Schwartztol

> work
> to heal this
> battered
> angry
> dysfunctional world
>
> So that
> you will
> find safety
> and sanity
> I promise
> to march
> and sign
> petitions
> and speak
> the truths
> that must
> surely triumph
> for you

For Isabella on her First Birthday

Watched a slide show
tonight of pictures
of your first year up
to now.
And I marveled
at your beauty.
your bright
savvy eyes
filled with
such wonder
and such joy.

And I watched
how all who
hold you
behold your
precious special
glow.

You are
so very loved
by your besotted
Daddy whose love
shines through
every encounter from
your very first days as

Holly W. Schwartztol

he holds you in awe
and wonder…
whether you are dancing
together or drumming
your own special
father daughter beat.

Your dearest mother's
rapt attention to you…
her tenderness
spills through as she
holds you close
gazing at you
or sharing you
with Auntie Danielle
Grandma and Grandpa
Uncle Mikey and Uncle Andrew.
Sam and Ella sparkle
as if they knew
the secret of your
dearness.
and Auntie Jill
shares special laughter
with you and your Mommy.

You light up with Safta Ziva
and your two grandpas
your expressions
beam a knowing

of understanding
much more than
you can tell us yet.

For sure you
light up all our lives
with your laughter
as you clap your hands
or "read" your books or
model your pretty clothes.

And, so dear Izzie
Isabella or whatever
you finally call
yourself when you
have a say...
this is simply
your Grandma's way
of saying
Happy happy First Birthday!

Holly W. Schwartztol

Written after seeing the Sonogram of grandchild:

Dear baby someone
you are a
mere 8 weeks
old and so
I cannot yet
shout from the
rooftops about you.

But, I love you
so and your
picture is sublime
waiting for the time
when I can show
it off to all.

For now there
is something special
and sweet about
keeping you under
wraps of just the family
and one friend.

Along My Garden Path

Years from now
I will show you
how much your
Grandma loved you
from the moment
I learned of your
impending arrival

Holly W. Schwartztol

For Baby Grandson Schwartztol

In just a few
short
weeks
baby grandson
Schwartztol

Whose first
name remains
a closely kept
secret within

Held dear by
your parents
and yet soon
to be a full
fledged member
of the
burgeoning family clan.

We've glimpsed your face in
the sonogram
just a tiny
preview of
the you
we soon
will hold

Along My Garden Path

Not only in our
arms but in
the deepest parts
 of our beings

And so this poem
which I write on
the 2nd of May
2018 is my
message to
You

Which one day
years from now
you may read
and know
how much we
love you

Holly W. Schwartztol

NAMED IN UTERO

Lafayette and Tallulah
they didn't mean
to fool ya

Names so well suited
for nine months
til you were booted

out to the
stratosphere where
 you're hanging out

Never forgotten
but now is your fate
to be simply known as
Isabella and Nate

CELEBRATE
GOOD THINGS

Holly W. Schwartztol

When You Just Know

It's more than lust
or simple attraction
I knew I must
enter this transaction

A hasty decision
to some it might seem
my life in transition
in forming this team

We must have known
from a past life connection
this other one
was a tasty confection

We took the chance
married very soon
we're still doing our dance
we're still over the moon

Reunion, 2009

It's June and they're calling
curiosity's enthralling
it's Reunion time again

Do we really dare
to go back there
with our eyes and minds open?

Or do we shun
what was begun
and feign disinterest and ennui?

To finally discover
inklings that hover
evoking our hidden selves

Previously published in Dalton Alumni Magazine

Holly W. Schwartztol

For Carolyn Garwood, PhD, On her Retirement

Back in 1973
she was introduced
to me
A lovely
Hepburnish
lady in a
small office
lined with books.

I wanted her
to admit me
to the program
and welcomed her
encouragement
to apply…

It was in her class
where we fashioned
our coats of arms
as the fledgling therapists
we hoped to be.
The years of school
brought challenges
and those many
hoops we leapt through.

Amidst all the
ups and downs
and more
Carolyn's
face shined
through
as a beacon
assuring us
how surely one
day we'd
complete that
thorny doctorate.

But way beyond
the years of school
Carolyn has been
a friend to me
and to so many
others.

From lunches at
Captain's Tavern
or attending my
book signings at Books & Books
she's listened
to all my
adventures always
with that clear
headedness

Holly W. Schwartztol

which never
judged.
Her head
turning characteristically
as she tried
to understand
what path
I might be on
that month
or year.

So truly,
Carolyn has been
a mentor
a friend
and a cherished
witness to my
career as it
blossomed
and even now
when I have closed
up shop
and moved on.

I trust these lines
suffice to applaud
and thank you,
dearest Carolyn
for all you are
and how you've been
to so many of us.

In Love with the Sea

How happy are we
in our home by the sea
gazing at the ocean
fills us with sweet notion

Some days the waves churl
in a fit of a whirl
on serene days the wake
becomes the Atlantic Lake

Our walks along the shore
thrill us to our core
as birds gather at our feet
nothing is more sweet

We're completely smitten
with our home so it's fittin'
to praise this great locale
of Cape Canaveral

Holly W. Schwartztol

Anniversary 2016

Sunlight softly kissed the sidewalks
on that sweet November Sunday
as hand in hand we entered
the Long Island Temple
where we gently
promised in front
of family and friends
that we'd love each
other always.

Joan Baez on the tape
strains of Windsong
as the daughter
in her party dress
made her way down
the aisle
followed by us
two and everyone
knew by the broad
smiles we wore
that this match
was one for the ages.

It's November again
41 years later
and we still
are smiling
the sun shines
in Florida and
we two are
still smiling
looking back at
all we've been
for each other
richer still for
all these years.

He lights up
my life just
as he did in
1975 and we
celebrate our
love grown
deeper for the
passing of time.

Holly W. Schwartztol

Along My Garden Path

Amazing Grace

Holly W. Schwartztol

Dragonfly

For near twenty
years you've called to me

with special messages
sometimes of wonder
and others of warning

Seems when first
you and I connected
no one else claimed

you for their own
and I cherished your
delicate clarity as mine

alone as my
ambassador
of good or bad will

and I knew not
in those early days
of the variety of

your beauty and
ethereal qualities
only that you spoke

Along My Garden Path

to me when I
needed to hear
what you were

bringing as you
flew near me
hovering as a

perfect creature
in my garden
or by the seaside

and those who
know me well
bring me

jewels of your
perfect dragonfly
essence

Holly W. Schwartztol

Special Codes

Leonard Cohen's lingering voice
speaks volumes to me
he's no longer earthbound
yet I wonder if he has the choice

to connect with my vibration
and feel my emotions
the deepest of connections
some sadness, some elation

John Denver's country roads
elicit my yearnings
he's on the other side
are there some special codes

that link their hearts to mine
so they receive my message
as I connect with theirs
as humanly divine?

Our Safe Oasis

We gather
for meditation at
Sandy's sweet house
set among the trees

Week after week
sharing stories
on our journeys
to spirit and back

At Sandy's we
bare our souls
and listen to
the small voice

Within as we
welcome our guides
and ancestors
who support us

As we search
within ourselves
and as we reach
out to one another

Holly W. Schwartztol

From the joining
to the guided meditations
bringing our authentic selves
we intently tune in

Giving support and comfort
or celebrating our joys
knowing we are safe
in our explorations

An oasis where
truths are bared
amid the safety
and solace of spirit

Lines of Communication

Once it was
The medium was the message
then the messages
came from Mediums

They say the veil
is thinning and
our loved ones
will not fail

To find means of reaching
of joining with us here
as we open to the teaching
in this earthly sphere

Just in the next dimension
we've only to pay attention
not be afraid to mention
we've got the right extension

If they were away on vacation
or in on an excavation
we'd not think it one bit odd
we'd expect to receive a nod

Holly W. Schwartztol

The subtle lines they're sending
ask only we not ignore
and allow old beliefs upending
as they reach deep into our core

For we're swiftly discerning
as our thoughts are turning
and as our minds open
Mediumship is there for learning

Meditation is the key
for them to come through
as we let our hearts be
open to their subtle hue

Don't ignore the signs
and cause them much frustration
just open to their lines
of spirit communication

In Another Dimension

In another dimension
in another place
with no thought to intention
we first met face to face.

But what's the meaning of time
when worlds dissolve in minutes
the feeling's oh so sublime
feelings transcend the limits

These unconscious connections
reaching from there to here
in so many directions
making far away near

In another dimension
in another place
with no thought to intention
we first met face to face.

Holly W. Schwartztol

ACKNOWLEDGMENTS

My husband, Robert, has urged me to publish my poems in a book and now I've finally listened to him. Although he likes my novels, he is especially enthusiastic about my poetry.

My friend, Pat Gallant Weich, has been my poetry muse for many years. With her encouragement, I entered poems in the Faulkner Society Writing Competition and have been delighted to see many of them receive recognition. Pat has been a wonderful source for helping me fine-tune some of my poems.

Dr. Sharon Wesch and Julie Goldsmith Gilbert gave their time to help me finalize the manuscript.

I was delighted to work with my illustrator, Vincent Ostertag. I've enjoyed brainstorming with Vince about ways to enhance the book with his intuitive drawings.

John Prince, of Hallard Press, assisted in the organization of the poems and has been very helpful all through the process of preparing the book.

My friends have listened to my poems for decades and have also encouraged me to publish a collection.

As always, my children Larry, Andrew and Jill and their spouses, Daphna Renan, May Flam and John Caplan have been very supportive.

About the Author

Holly W Schwartztol is a poet, novelist, teacher and retired psychologist. She finds poems tend to present themselves and she has to write them down immediately. Her poems have placed in the Faulkner writing competition for over four years.

Holly has written three novels: *Sherry and the Unseen World* (2005), *What We Tell* (2012) and *Coming Around Again* (2019).

She consults with other authors, encouraging them to find their unique voices and is a popular teacher of memoir writing. When not writing, Holly spends time doing jigsaw puzzles, crossword puzzles, singing, studying mediumship, and talking with her lifelong friends.

A past president of several professional organizations including the South Florida Writers Association (SFWA), The Dade County Psychological Association (Holly holds a PhD in Psychology) and the Florida Society of Clinical Hypnosis, she serves as an editor of *Authors Voice,* the monthly publication of SFWA.

Holly lives in eastern Florida with her husband, Robert. They have three children and five grandchildren. She leads book club discussions of her books and poetry—during the pandemic on Zoom and on Free Conference Call. Contact her at DrHollySchwartztol@Yahoo.com.

About the Illustrator

Vincent Ostertag is a multi-media artist and musician with a background in television and film. A painter and sculptor, Vincent is currently a contract artist in the theme park industry in the Orlando, Florida area.

Holly W. Schwartztol

Other Books by the Author

Coming Around Again, GoMyStory.com, 2019

What We Tell, iuniverse, 2012

Sherry and the Unseen World, iuniverse, 2005

In A Darkness, with James A. Wechsler and Nancy F. Wechsler, first edition, Norton, 1972; Second Edition, Pickering Press, 1988